Super Safari 2

Activity Book

T0349660

Herbert Puchta   Günter Gerngross   Peter Lewis-Jones

CAMBRIDGE
UNIVERSITY PRESS

Shaftesbury Road, Cambridge CB2 8EA, United Kingdom

One Liberty Plaza, 20th Floor, New York, NY 10006, USA

477 Williamstown Road, Port Melbourne, VIC 3207, Australia

314–321, 3rd Floor, Plot 3, Splendor Forum, Jasola District Centre, New Delhi – 110025, India

103 Penang Road, #05-06/07, Visioncrest Commercial, Singapore 238467

Cambridge University Press & Assessment is a department of the University of Cambridge.

We share the University's mission to contribute to society through the pursuit of education, learning and research at the highest international levels of excellence.

www.cambridge.org
Information on this title: www.cambridge.org/9781107476899

First published 2015

40 39 38 37 36 35 34 33 32 31

Printed in the Netherlands by Wilco BV

A catalogue record for this publication is available from the British Library

ISBN 978-1-107-47689-9 Activity Book Level 2
ISBN 978-1-107-47688-2 Pupil's Book with DVD-ROM Level 2
ISBN 978-1-107-47690-5 Teacher's Book Level 2
ISBN 978-1-107-47704-9 Teacher's DVD
ISBN 978-1-107-47691-2 Class Audio CDs Level 2
ISBN 978-1-107-47692-9 Flashcards Level 2
ISBN 978-1-107-47699-8 Presentation Plus DVD-ROM Level 2
ISBN 978-1-107-53927-3 Big Book Level 2
ISBN 978-1-107-49662-0 Posters Level 2
ISBN 978-1-107-47732-2 Puppet

Additional resources for this publication at www.cambridge.org/supersafari

Super Safari 2 Activity Book

Hello!

1 Look and match. Say the names.

1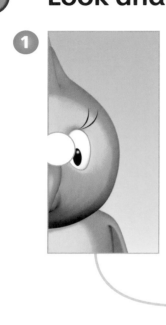

2

3

4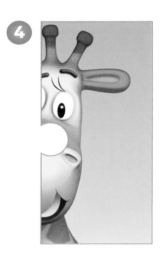

2 Draw yourself. Say the sentences.

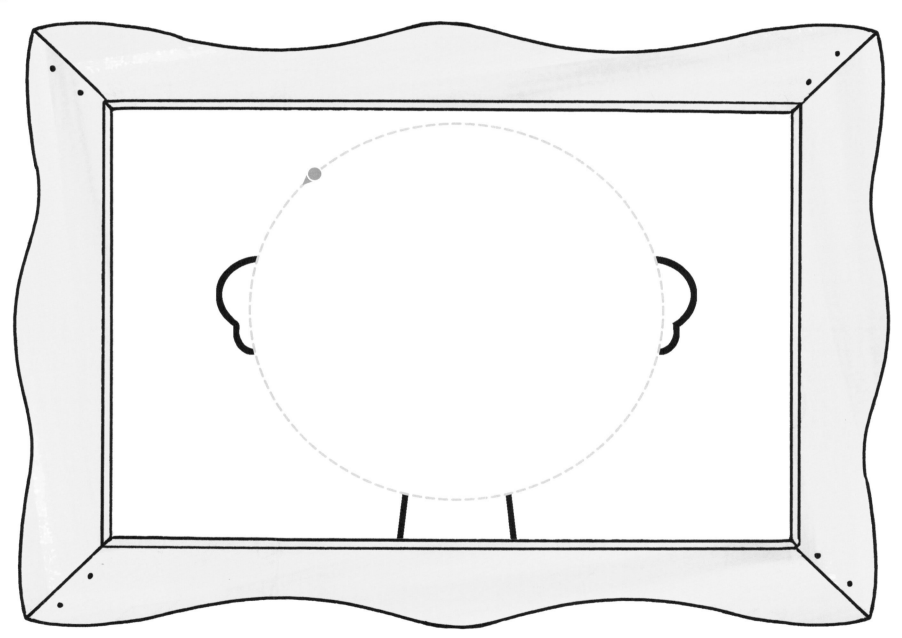

3 CD1 06 **Listen and circle.**

1

2

4 Say the names. Colour the circles.

1

2

3

4

1 Look, find and circle. Say the words.

1

2

3

4

5

6

board, paper, computer, desk, crayon, pencil case

2 CD1 11 **Listen and circle. Say the sentences.**

1

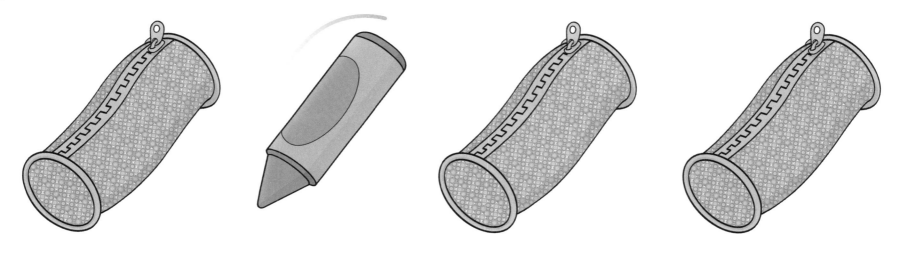

2

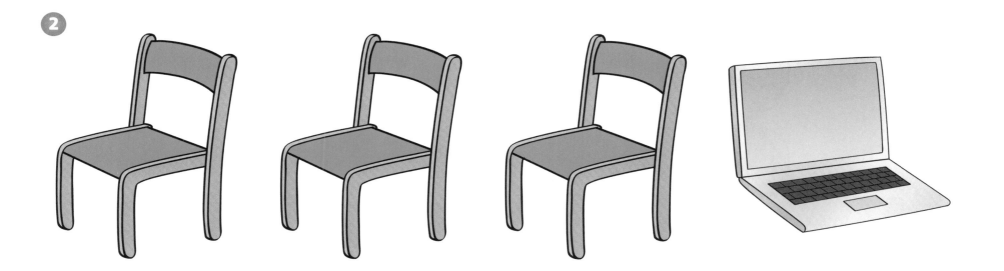

This is my (crayon). 9

3 Listen and circle.

1

2

4 CD1 17 **Listen again. Colour and complete.**

Listen and colour the correct circles.

1

2

6 Complete the faces (☺ or ☹). Colour the pictures.

7 **Make a bowling game.**

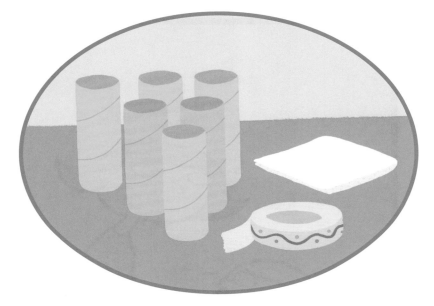

1

2

3

8 Say the words. Colour the circles.

1

2
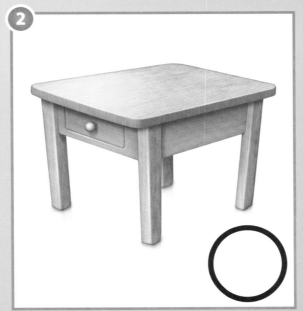

3

4

5

6

2 My body

2 **Listen, trace and match. Say the sentences.**

I can (clap my hands). 17

Listen and circle.

1

2

4 CD1 32 **Listen again and trace.**

Listen and colour the correct circles.

1

2

6 **Complete the faces (☺ or ☹). Colour the pictures.**

7 **Make a self-portrait.**

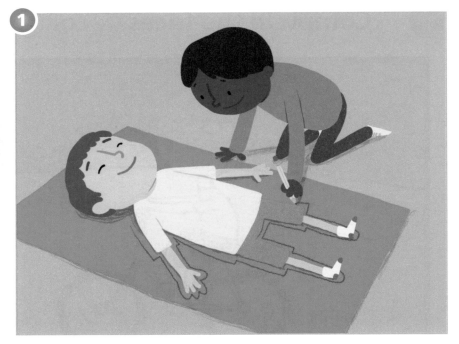

8 Say the words. Colour the circles.

1

2

3

4

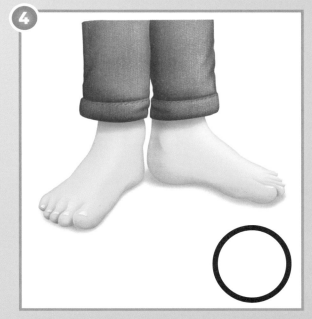

5

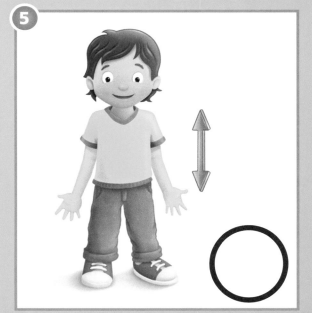

6

3 My room

1 Look, trace and colour. Say the words.

toy box, bookcase, lamp, mat, window, door

2 CD1 39 **Listen and colour. Say the sentences.**

1

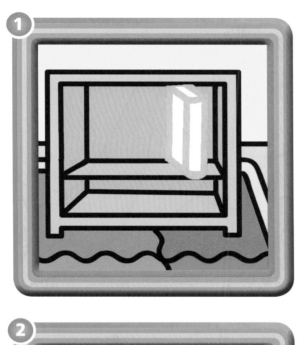

2

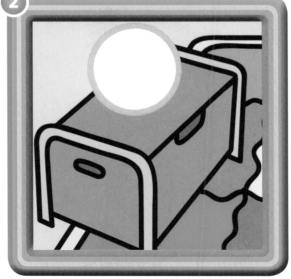

3

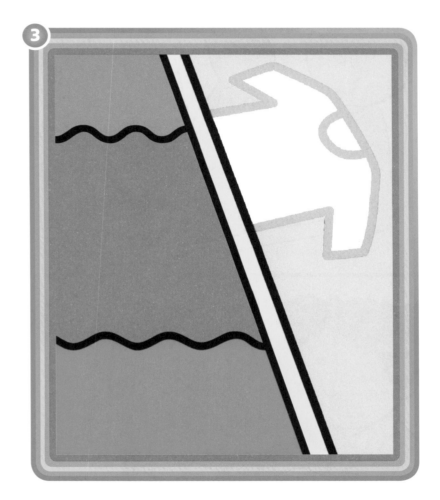

Listen and circle.

1

2

4 CD1 45 Listen again. Draw your room.

CD1 47 **Listen and colour the correct circles.**

1

2

6 Complete the faces (☺ or ☹). Colour the pictures.

7 **Make a poster of your room.**

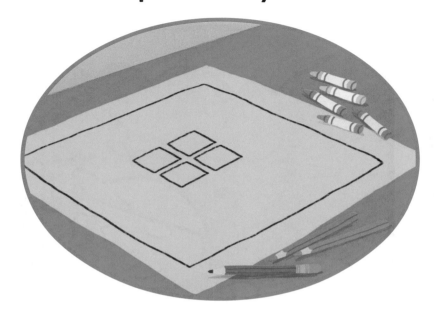

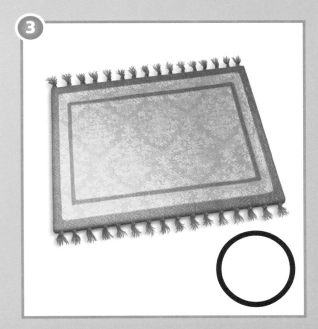

8 Say the words. Colour the circles.

1

2

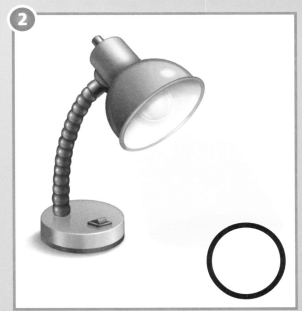

3

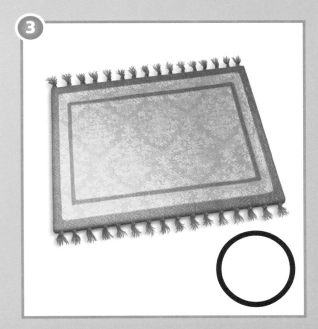

4

5

6

4 In the jungle

1 CD1 52 **Listen and circle. Say the animals.**

1

2

rhino, tiger, elephant, snake, spider, crocodile

2 CD1 54 Listen and join the dots. Say the sentences.

Listen and circle.

1

2

4 CD1 60 **Listen again. Follow and trace.**

Listen and colour the correct circles.

1

◯ ◯

2

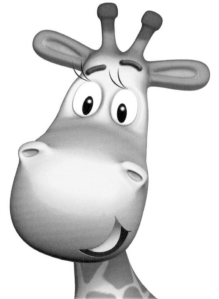 

◯ ◯

6 **Complete the faces (☺ or ☹). Colour the pictures.**

7 Make a jungle collage.

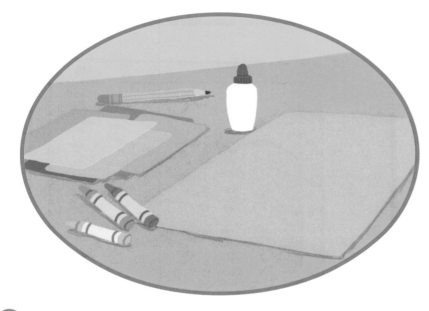

8 Say the animals. Colour the circles.

1

2
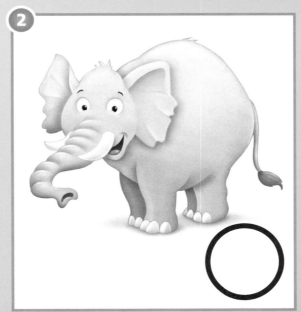

3
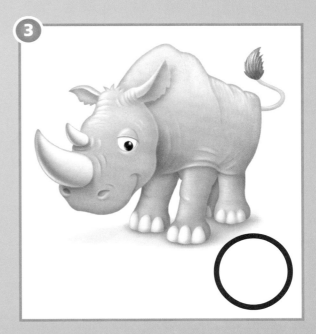

4

5

6

5 Fruit and vegetables

1 CD1 66 **Listen and match. Count and say the food.**

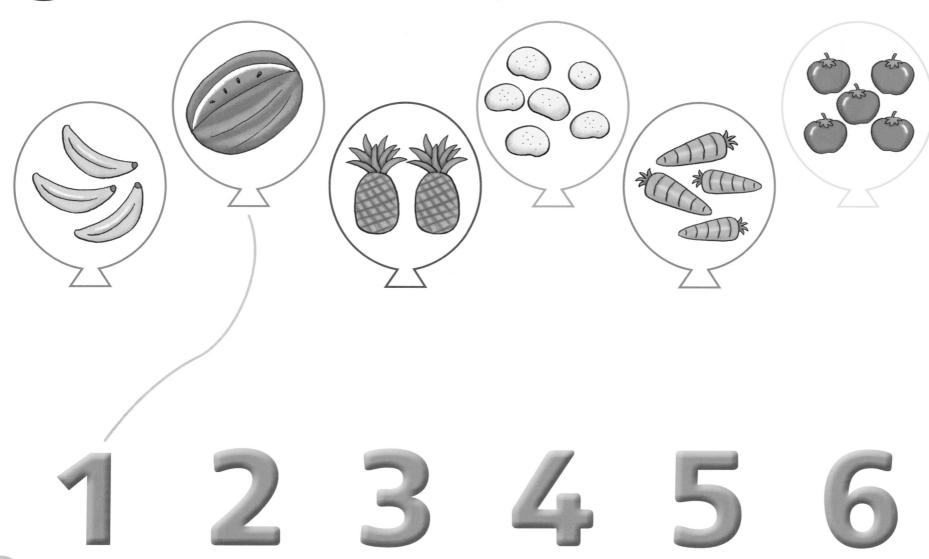

potatoes, pineapple, carrots, tomatoes, watermelon, bananas

2 **Draw lines to the food you** ♡ **and** 🚫**.**

3 **Listen and circle.**

1

2

4 **Listen again. Match and say the words.**

1

2

5 **Listen and colour the correct circles.**

1

2

6 Complete the faces (☺ or ☹). Colour the pictures.

7 Make a fruit and vegetable print poster.

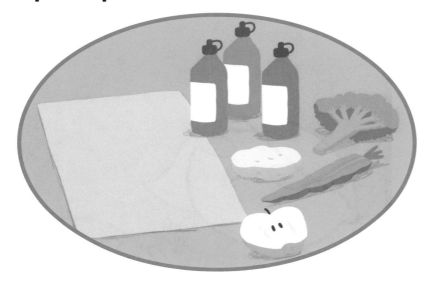

8 Say the words. Colour the circles.

1

2

3

4

5

6

6 My town

1 **Look and circle. Say the places.**

1

2

3

bus stop, park, school, toy shop, supermarket, zoo

2   **Look and follow the paths. Trace and say the sentences.**

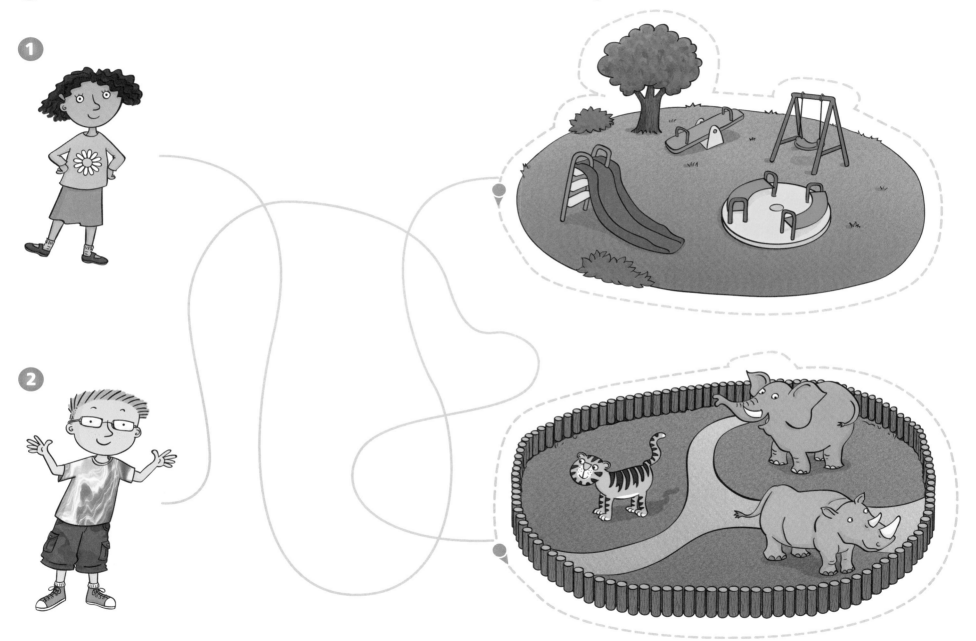

3 **Listen and circle.**

1

2

4 **Listen again. Draw your town.**

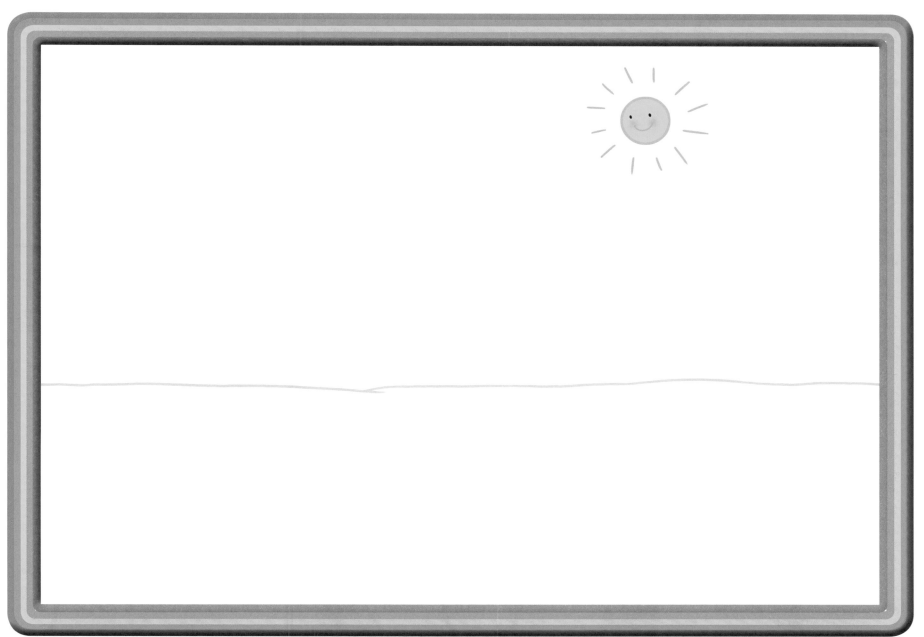

5 **Listen and colour the correct circles.**

1

2

6 Complete the faces (☺ or ☹). Colour the pictures.

7 Make a recycling poster.

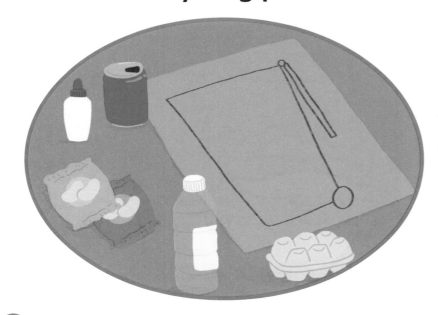

8 **Say the places. Colour the circles.**

1

2

3

4

5

6

1 Look and circle the odd one out. Say the jobs.

1

2

3

farmer, police officer, builder, doctor, firefighter, teacher

2 CD2 27 **Listen, trace and match. Say the sentences.**

1

2

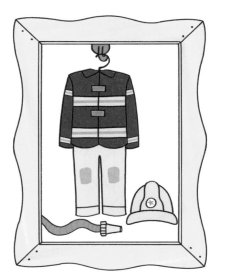

Listen and circle.

1

2

4 CD2 33 **Listen again. Trace and colour.**

 **CD2 35** Listen and colour the correct circles.

1

2

6 Complete the faces (☺ or ☹). Colour the pictures.

7 Make a fire engine costume.

1

2

3

8 Say the jobs. Colour the circles.

1

2

3

4

5

6

8 The weather

1 Look and match. Say the weather.

rainy, windy, cold, snowy, hot, sunny

2 **Look and trace. Say the sentences.**

3 **CD2 43** **Listen and circle.**

1

2

4 CD2 46 **Listen again. Trace and match.**

1

2

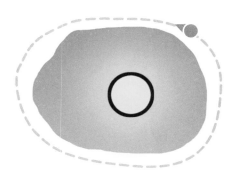

Listen and colour the correct circles.

1

2

6 Complete the faces (☺ or ☹). Colour the pictures.

7 **Make a weather dial.**

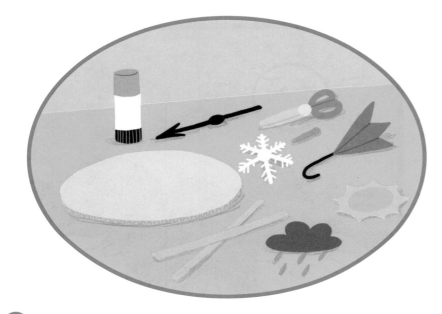

8 **Say the weather. Colour the circles.**

1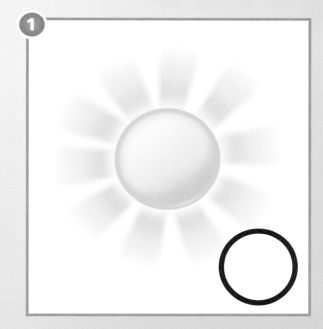

2

3

4

5

6

9 In the countryside

1 What's next? Match and say the words.

1

2

3

72 tree, leaves, frog, grass, flower, bee

2 ^{CD2}₅₃ **Listen and trace. Say the sentences.**

1

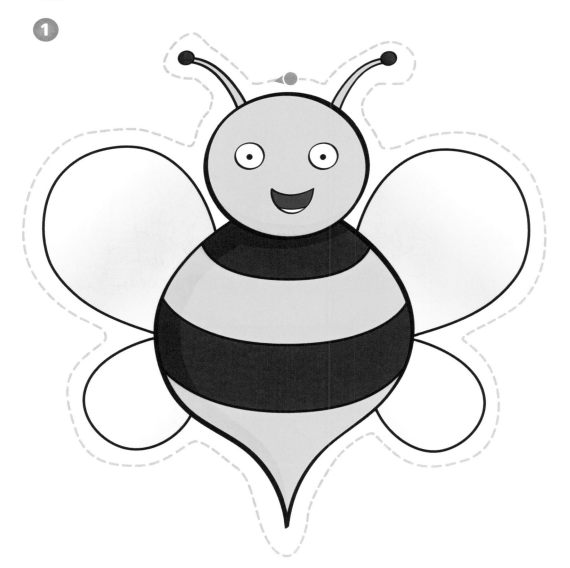

2

The (bee) is / isn't (small). It's (big). **73**

1

2

4 **Listen again. Trace and colour.**

5 **Listen and colour the correct circles.**

1

2

6 Complete the faces (☺ or ☹). Colour the pictures.

7 **Make a pond collage.**

8 **Say the words. Colour the circles.**

1

2

3

4

5

6

dad

cat

pin

sit

pen

bed

pot

dot

bus

cut

mat

mum

job

jam

lamp

log

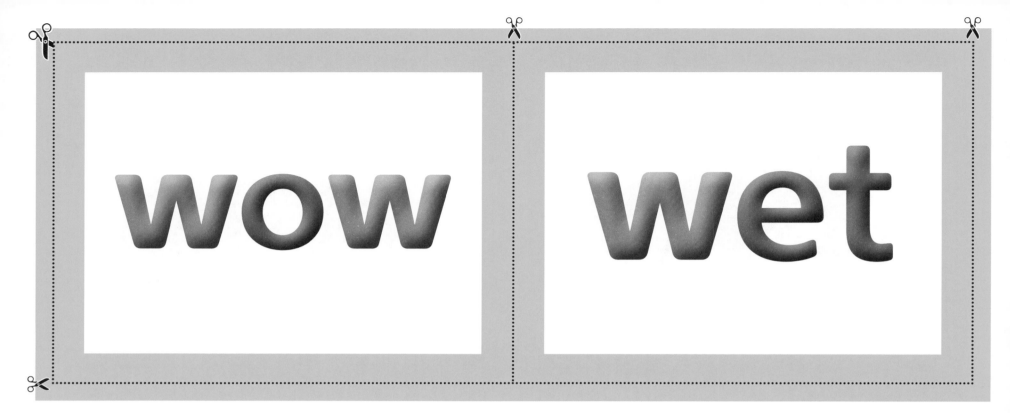

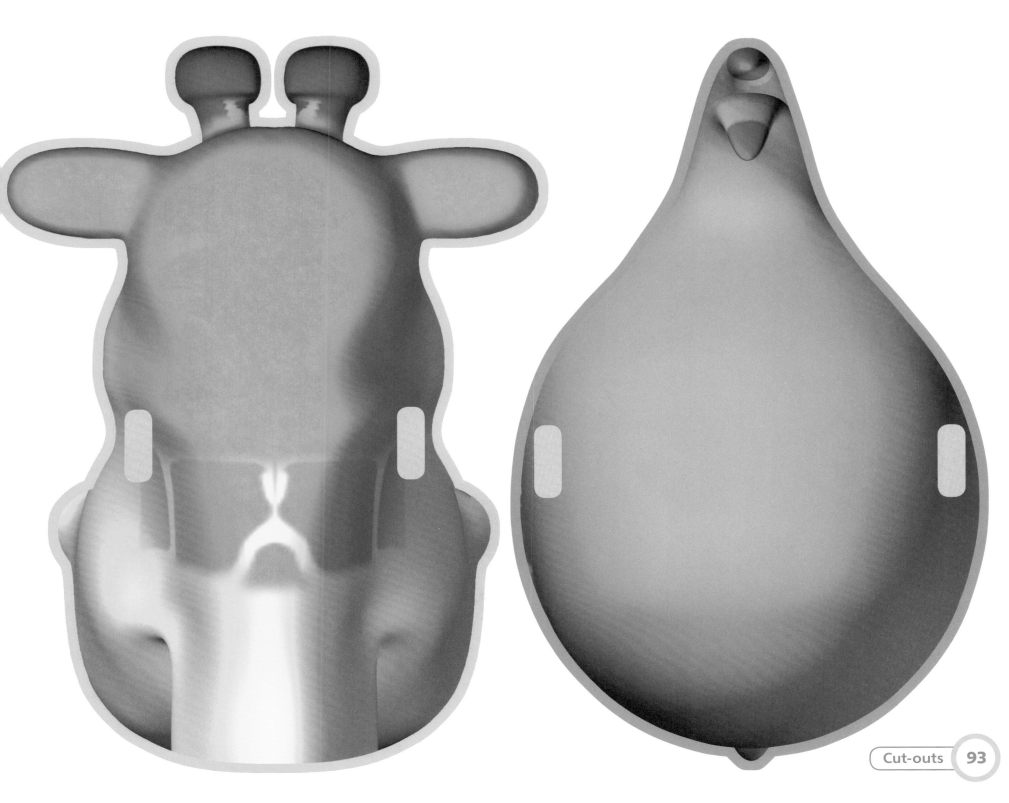

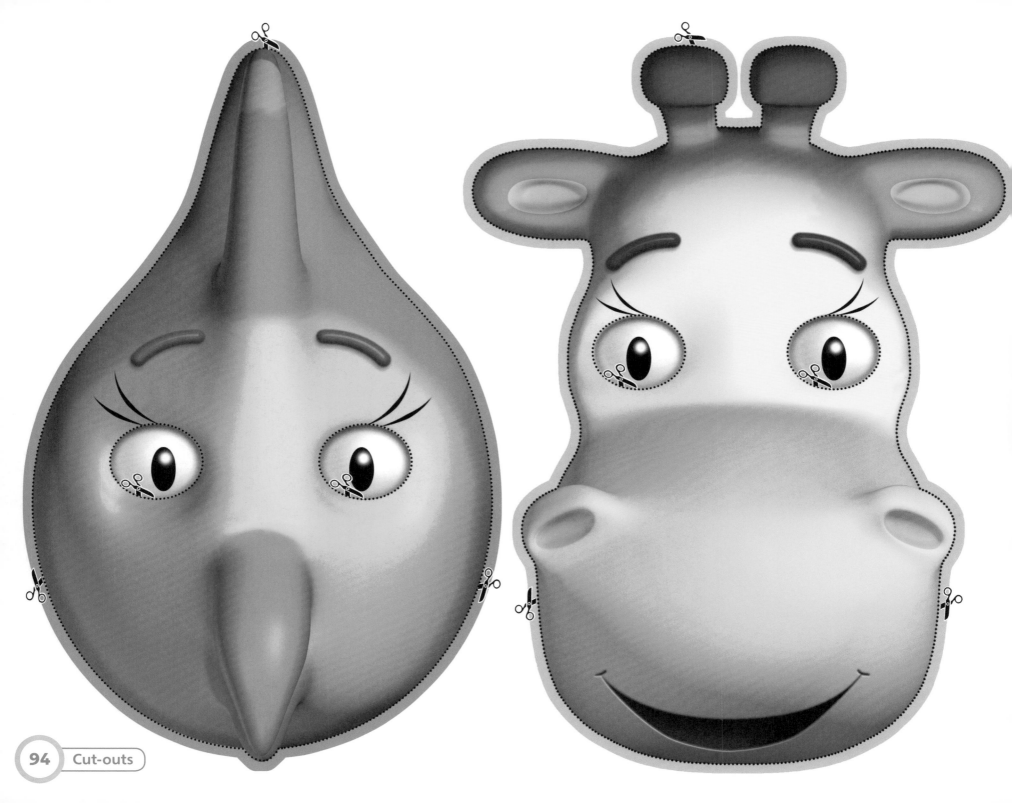

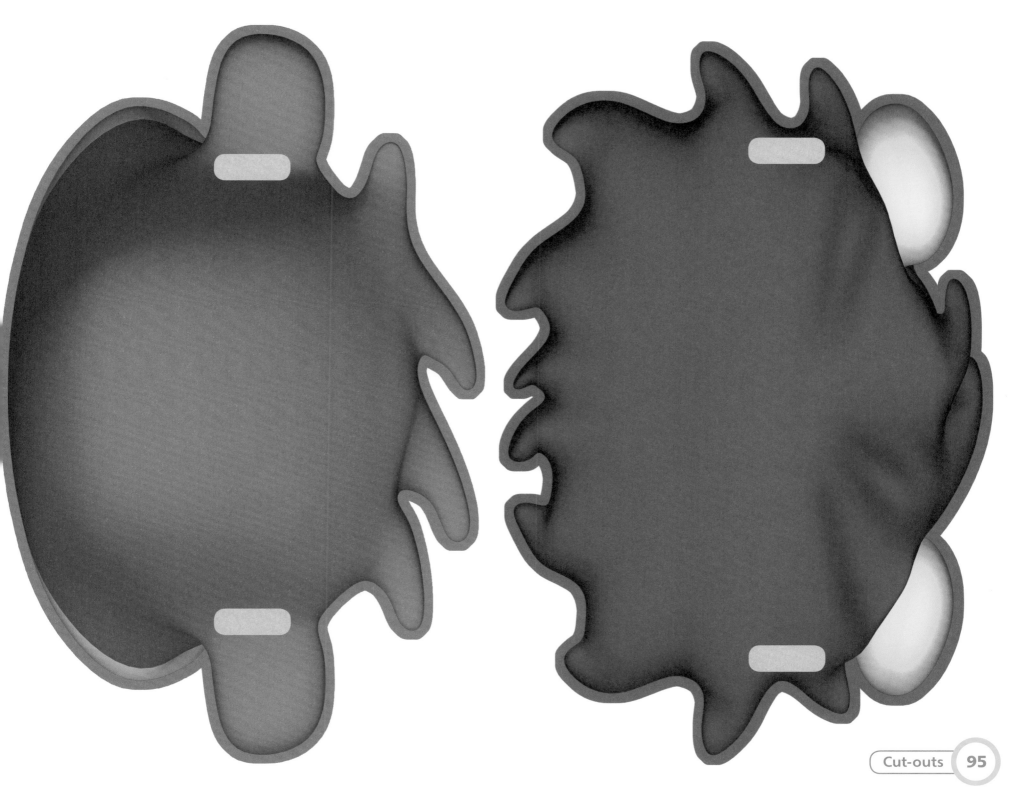

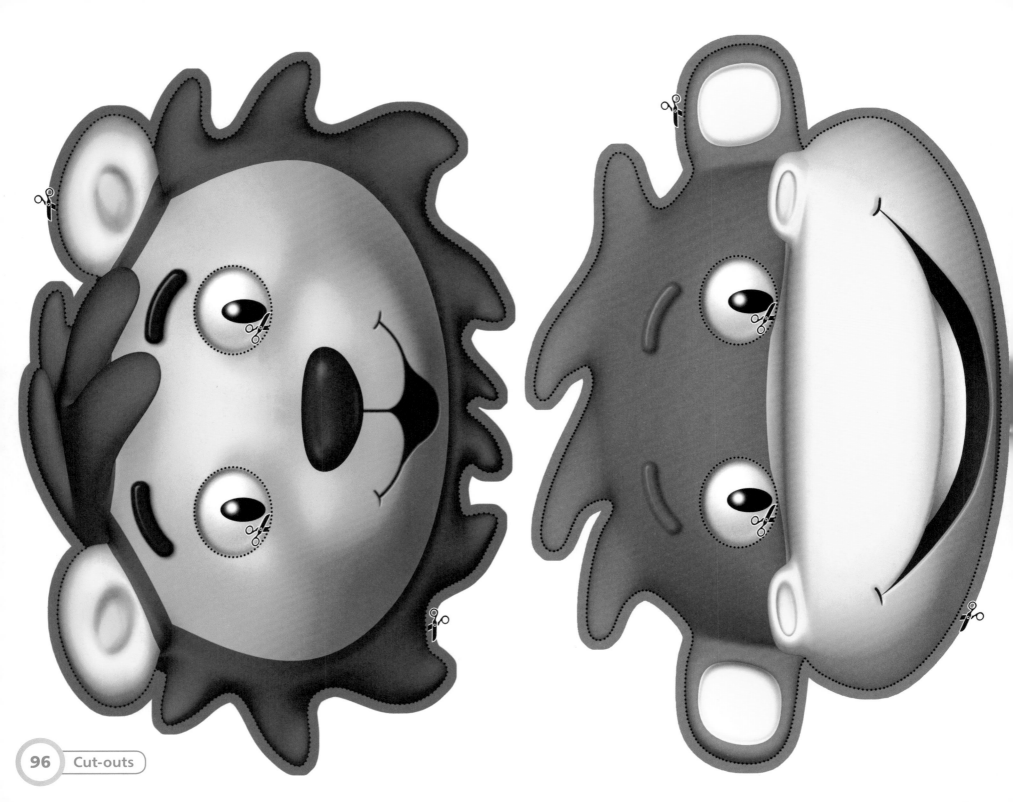